PRAISE FOR *SUPERPOWER*

"'Are you a giraffe?' This might just be one of the most powerful questions ever asked. Yet, knowing who we are is only the first step. Positively walking in and living out our TRUTH is where the magic happens. *Superpower* is a story that inspires us at any age to FIND and DISCOVER our inimitable superpower, to LOVE and EMBRACE our uniqueness, and to CONFIDENTLY and JOYFULLY show the world our AUTHENTIC self!"
—**Heather Dias,** ACC, Transformational Life Coach, CPC, ACC, ELI-MP, Author, Trainer, Speaker

"The book's message applies to so many—kids and adults alike. The idea of being inimitable is incredibly intriguing and makes one think about their own superpower and how they might use that to help themselves and others. The insight provided allows the reader to easily relate and hopefully gain a better understanding of themself. This book has the ability to change not only someone's mindset, but also can empower one to do and be better. Very inspiring. A fast and meaningful read!"
—**Bre Bjerketvedt,** Secondary Teacher, St. Michael

Superpower

Superpower

**AN INSPIRING STORY TO
OVERCOME SELF-DOUBT
AND UNLEASH
YOUR AUTHENTIC GREATNESS**

KATE LEAVELL

Bestselling Coauthor of *Stick Together*

WILEY

Published by John Wiley & Sons, Inc., Hoboken, New Jersey.
Published simultaneously in Canada.

Illustrations by Jay Schwartz.

For general information on our other products and services or for technical support, please contact our Customer Care Department within the United States at (800) 762-2974, outside the United States at (317) 572-3993 or fax (317) 572-4002.

Wiley also publishes its books in a variety of electronic formats. Some content that appears in print may not be available in electronic formats. For more information about Wiley products, visit our web site at www.wiley.com.

Library of Congress Cataloging-in-Publication Data is Available:

ISBN: 9781119890430 (cloth)
ISBN: 9781119890447 (ePub)
ISBN: 9781119890454 (ePDF)

COVER ART & DESIGN: PAUL MCCARTHY

SKY10033602_061322

This book is dedicated to my amazing kiddos, Michael, Drew, and Meredith. Thank you for sharing your superpowers with me. You each are an inimitable gift to this world, and you inspire me every day.

Contents

Acknowledgments

I had to first take the journey to learn acceptance and love of myself before I could write this book. The inner work I had to do was the hardest part, and I never could have transformed and embraced life the way I have without the love and support of so many amazing people in my life. My grandfather, Albert Conord, passed away while I was editing the final copy and as I sat at his funeral I was flooded with gratitude for including the character of Mr. E's dad that was inspired by the conversations I've had with him. I want to thank my dad; my brother, Dave; and my sister, Sarah; for always being at the ready when I need help or late-night edits. Trent, the original Mr. Inimitable, this story was inspired by your infatuation with the word *inimitable* and the way you live your life unapologetically true to yourself. Jon Gordon, there aren't enough pages to express the gratitude I have for you and your mentorship; your family; your awesome and supportive wife, Kathryn; your friendship; and for believing in me even when I sometimes struggled to believe in myself. Thank you for every amazing opportunity and for believing in *Stick Together*. Janine Tucker, I don't have words to thank you for how you've gone above and beyond for me and my baby girl; you are an amazing mentor and human. Special love and shoutout to the Jon Gordon Team: you are truly my family. Thank you to my loyal supporters, clients, followers, and mentors, your encouragement has kept me going. To Bill, you are inimitable in every way and I'm so much better for it. Your inspiring ability to persevere in any circumstance, your limitless encouragement, and your relentless belief in me gave me the strength to finish this project and keep chasing my dreams.

Introduction

"Mr. Inimitable, tell us again how you got your nickname," said Michael as they walked out to the soccer field. The other students joined in asking to hear the story again, one of their favorites to listen to.

Mr. Inimitable, also known as Coach Trent to his beloved team and students, smiled as he remembered the day he learned exactly who he is and, more important, what his superpower is. He thought of his beloved teacher Mr. E, who had affected his life so much and was never far from his mind. He looked at the building of this amazing school that changed his life and his perspective, and is now the very same building where he loves to teach and coach the boys' and girls' soccer teams.

"Okay, after practice, I'll leave a little extra time and I'll tell it to you again. But the deal is, after I tell you the story, you all have to share what your own superpowers are with the team!"

The kids walked a little faster to the field knowing they would get to hear the story again soon. But Meredith looked down at her feet. She wasn't sure if she had a superpower to share. What if Mr. Inimitable found out she was just like everyone else? She tried to push it out of her mind and focus on practicing one of her favorite sports. Mr. Inimitable was the best soccer coach she ever had, and it was hard to feel negative for long when he was on the field with them!

Before the warm-up was even over, Meredith had forgotten all about story time after practice. She was the first one to grab a ball and start working on her dribbling skills around every cone as tight as she could. Meredith was always the first one on the field and one of the hardest and most positive workers on the team. But she didn't think she was as good as the other players on her team because she didn't score a lot of goals.

As practice ended, and the group began to surround Mr. Inimitable, sitting on the ground to hear the story, Meredith started to feel nervous again.

"Okay, guys, it started before I ever set foot inside this school. I remember moving day like it was yesterday," Coach Trent began.

Inimitable: adj; So good or unusual as to be impossible to copy; unique.

Enigma: noun; A person or thing that is mysterious, puzzling, or difficult to understand; a riddle.

Superpower

Chapter One

Moving Day

There was hardly space to get comfortable in the back seat with every square inch of the car filled with anything and everything that didn't fit into the moving truck. A floor lamp and a mop pole divided the backseat between Trent and Emma. A stack of books, pillows, and blankets were piled up on the seat propping up the poles, and the two siblings took turns trying to shove the pile a little farther away from their own side.

It was another move. Trent was used to the process of packing, driving, unpacking, rearranging rooms, and eating takeout for a week while mom tried to find all the dishes.

"This is the last move, guys," promised their dad as they had brought the boxes back out of the garage to tape together again. But he had said that the time before, too. Trent heard him talking to some of his friends one night about being on a fast track to success and expanding territories, whatever that meant. He just knew that for him it meant moving every time a new city launched new stores, and they were on move number 6.

Even though Trent was used to moving, he never got used to starting all over at a new school. He had a really hard time making friends, so when he would make one and then have to leave, it was really hard to say goodbye. He tried to stay in touch with his friends at each place, but he wasn't really there long enough to create long-lasting bonds and eventually they stopped messaging.

Trent had another worry. A big one. Every school he went to he had to deal with the teasing, bullying, and laughing over the one thing he desperately wanted to hide. Having to face another group of kids who were going to tease him was almost too much to imagine. He slid down in his seat and turned up his music to drown out his thoughts.

He glanced over at Emma, dancing in her seat with her pink headphones and coloring in her doodle notebook. She loved moving. He couldn't understand it. How did she not have to deal with the same bullying he did? He could think of a list of things to make fun of her about right now off the top of his head. After all, she was his little sister.

Chapter Two

Can You Hear Me?

Deep inside of a dream while he dozed off in the backseat, Trent's fears about the new school brought painful memories back to the surface.

"Hey, new kid, can you hear me NOW?" "HOW ABOUT NOW!" came the voices from behind him getting louder and louder. He tried to speed up to get away but as he started to create some distance, other voices came from all sides of him.

"Slow down, you're creating a windstorm!" called out one of the voices, followed by a burst of laughter.

And then, seemingly out of nowhere, came Mrs. Jenkins, his third-grade teacher. She walked right in front of him and suddenly he found himself sitting at his desk looking right up at her face. She leaned in and said with an irritated tone, "Trent, did you hear me? Joe can't see the board. Can you move your desk to the left so he can see around you?"

The room filled with laughs and more comments that he couldn't make out because of the blood rushing to his head with embarrassment.

The room started to get dark and his desk was bumping around a lot. *What's going on?* he thought.

"HONKKKKKK" came a loud horn from the car behind him as Trent bolted awake in his seat still pressed up against the mop pole and the pile of books and blankets. Another bad dream. He was not looking forward to a new school. The faces changed but the teasing was always the same.

He pulled out his phone and turned on the camera to look at them again. Not that he needed to. He had it memorized, and they never changed. If only there was something he could do, all of his problems would go away. He made a decision right then and there that the new school was not going to see him like this. He would find a way to blend in and avoid being made fun of no matter what it took. Invisible Trent. *If only I could be a superhero with the power to disappear*, he thought.

"Hey, guys, look over there, it's your new school!" said their mom. "Looks like a really fun place, much better than your old one! And look, Emma, you'll be in the building right next door! You can walk home together!" Trent shot her a look that said, "You're joking, right?" And then he rested his head back against the seat to start doing some serious planning for becoming the most ordinary kid that the school would ever see.

Chapter Three

The Most Ordinary Kid Has His First Day of School

Trent grabbed a bowl and started pouring in his favorite cereal while pushing down a chocolate frosted pop tart into the toaster oven with his other hand. *Time for a healthy breakfast for the most ordinary kid ever*, he thought. This was what all the kids ate on the commercials, so he was already off to a great start.

His mom walked into the kitchen to grab her coffee. As she was saying good morning she stopped short in her tracks and did a double take, looking at Trent.

"Oh, umm, Trent, is that what you want to wear your first day at your new school?" she asked, trying to sound upbeat but ending with a nervous laugh. Trent looked over at his reflection in the window and shrugged. He thought it looked as ordinary as it could be. In fact, he could barely make out his reflection because it was so plain. *Plain and perfect*, he thought.

"Okay, well, grab Emma and walk her to school and make sure she gets checked in okay. I need to head out to work," she said, still wondering if she should tell him to go change back into his fun and quirky self that she loved so dearly. Trent loved to wear his favorite team's jerseys to school. He collected bright-colored sneakers and would match his whole outfit to the shoes. His personality was as big and fun as his outfits and he was always easy to find in a crowd. But today he was wearing plain jeans and a gray t-shirt and a plain gray hat that was too big. He didn't look like himself at all.

Trent shouted for Emma to come down to leave for school as he ran into the bathroom to get another look in the mirror. He put a sticky note on the mirror and repeated what it said over and over as he studied his reflection.

"You're the same as everyone else. There's nothing different about you at all."

He tugged his dad's old gray hat down a little more as he tucked his ears back against his head and tightened the strap in the back. They didn't stick out even a little bit. If he could just keep this hat on all day then no one would ever know he had the biggest, goofiest ears anyone had ever seen. Even his old basketball coach used to joke about the team fouling him by grabbing his "ear handles." The Jughead nickname stuck with him until they moved away.

Emma came bounding down the stairs wearing clothes that didn't match, a half-done braid, and a butterfly backpack that she stuffed with her tap shoes, "just in case." Trent shook his head. If she hadn't experienced bullying yet, today was the day it was going to start and then she would understand why moving isn't fun at all.

Chapter Four

Mr. E

"Okay, Trent, looks like you're all set, and you sure lucked out. You got Mr. E!" said the excited lady from the office who was getting his registration completed before he went to class.

Trent looked at her feeling a little confused and asked what the *E* stood for.

She smiled a big toothy grin and wound up her face ready to share her favorite story in the world to tell new students.

"Well," she said with a big breath, "we call him Mr. E or Mystery, which is what it sounds like when you say Mr. E. That's how we like to think of him because he is a very different sort of teacher. He's an enigma! Do you know what that is? Look it up; you'll be glad you did! He's the most beloved teacher by all the students and his last name is hard to say so we all started calling him Mr. E. But his real name is Mr. Enigmatic. It's very fitting because we just never know what he's going to do! As you can imagine, it's even harder to spell, so we stick with Mr. E."

"He sure is unique, you'll see!" she said, entirely too excited for a story that wasn't that amazing, thought Trent.

Trent's head was swirling. Unique? Different? Fun? And people loved him for that? He didn't believe it. *Not possible*, he thought. He can't be that different. Teachers are all the same. Trent took the hall map from the table and looked back at the office lady still grinning and now spinning around in her chair to some music playing in the background. *This sure is an unusual place*, thought Trent as he headed to his classroom with a stack of papers to bring home for his parents to fill out.

As he was rounding the corner, he heard her voice pop out from the office, "And, young man, no hats on inside the building, please and thank youuuuuuu," she sang out as chipper as could be. He turned and gave her a weak wave and a half smile. This hat was coming off only if someone pried it off his head, thought Trent. It was his only defense to the inevitable wave of taunts and laughter.

He got to the end of the hallway and looked at the map. He couldn't figure out which way was up. The map didn't make sense at all. He was starting to think this whole school was odd. As he studied the paper trying to find his classroom, a man approached him with a smile.

"Well hello there! Happy Friday, young man! Which way do you think you'll go?" Trent looked up and didn't know how to answer the question.

"Well, which way do you think most people go?" the man asked him.

"Oh, umm," Trent thought out loud as he looked left and right. There were more kids in the hallway to the right, so he pointed down that way. "That way?"

"Okay, then you should definitely go left!" smiled the man and then he whistled as he walked down the hallway to the office.

"Okay, umm, thanks," said Trent as he looked left and right again. This place was so weird! He looked left at the empty hallway and then turned right to the groups of kids laughing and walking somewhere with their bags. It made more sense to follow the other students; the other hallway looked deserted.

He followed close behind them as they walked through several hallways until he realized they were leaving out a backdoor and getting on a bus. Trent put his face in his hand and realized they were going on a field trip. He'd followed them all the way to the back of the school. Now he was really lost.

He heard whistling coming from down the hallway and he jogged back the way he came trying to find it. There was that man again, who clearly knew he was going to go right because he came to look for him.

"I thought you might try this way, come with me, you're in my class! I'm Mr. E!" said the man, offering him a fist bump. Trent bumped his fist and Mr. E did a dance move to finish it off. It made Trent laugh but he tried to hide it so he wouldn't look like he was having fun with a teacher in case anyone was watching. They headed down the hall to the classrooms and Trent braced for his first face-to-face with his class.

Before they walked in, Mr. E turned to Trent and said, "There's something you should know about my classroom. It's square and it has desks and it looks like every other classroom you've seen. But be aware that it's not like any other classroom you've ever been in. It's a MR. E classroom. It's an Enigma. It's like a puzzle. You get it?"

Trent nodded, but he had no idea what this odd teacher was talking about. Maybe he was just trying to distract him so he wouldn't be nervous. It wasn't working; his nerves were knotting up his stomach and creating a giant lump in his throat. To make matters worse, Mr. E then asked him if he would be alright with taking off his hat. Trent gave him a nervous look and shyly shook his head no.

"Oh, how mysterious," said his new teacher as he looked at him with heightened fascination. "Okay, very enigmatic, sir, I will allow it for now," Mr. E said and smiled as they walked in together.

Trent let out a deep breath he didn't realize he'd been holding and pulled his hat down tighter.

Chapter Five

Dinner Download

At Trent's house they had what their dad referred to as the "dinner download." If they couldn't all be at dinner together, they would do it before bed or over video chat. This was a time for each of them to share the adventures of their day. Trent looked over at Emma and could see she was already raising her hand and waving it around all over the place so she could share first. She usually got her way. Dad was on the iPad video chat propped up on the table streaming from his hotel in Dallas. It helped to see his family's faces but he was missing being home to share in the fun and connection in person.

Emma started rambling through the excitement of her first day of school. "I got to wear my tap shoes at lunch and they even let me get on one of the tables and do a tap dance, until I got caught and they made me get down and then I helped hand out papers, and collect books and I have three new best friends and they invited me to a movie night this weekend at their house and my teacher is so funny and she helped fix my braids, look!!" She gasped for a breath and then was about to continue when Trent interrupted her.

"No one said anything about your outfit? You didn't match at all! They didn't laugh at it?" asked Trent incredulously as he scanned her from head to toe. She looked like she got dressed in the dark. As this was Emma, she probably did; she didn't care what anyone thought.

Emma looked at her brother and laughed. "Oh, yeah, they thought it was funny! Some of the kids called me the new clown girl. I have a nickname already! This school is so fun!"

Trent shook his head. Nothing bothered her; he didn't get it. He reached up to rub his forehead where the hat had been digging in all day to keep his ears hidden and thought about having to wear that hat every day even when it got really hot and he wished he could find another way.

Trent handed the papers to his mom that she needed to fill out and told them all about Mr. E, the lady in the office, and his first day in his new class. Mr. E had handed him a puzzle piece to hang on the wall and told him to write his name on it. Trent hung it up next to all the other puzzle pieces that belonged to the other students. All around the puzzle pieces were giant question marks taped to the wall and a sign that read, "What is YOUR Superpower?" They were going to be working on their puzzle pieces all week, but Trent didn't understand what the project was all about yet. He was still worried about how long he could get away with wearing the hat every day.

He had managed to get through the entire day without too many people noticing him. He kept his hand down even though he knew the answers to the questions. He had some great ideas for the class discussion on a service project they could do over break, but he kept it to himself. Blend, blend, blend. He was pulling it off and he thought that just maybe, this could be the easiest move they'd ever done! He wore a satisfied smile all the way up to his room and used the weekend to stay focused on his plan.

Before he climbed into bed that night, Trent opened up the old worn-out dictionary his dad had given him and he looked up the meaning of enigma, like the chair-spinning lady in the front office had suggested. The definition read:

> Enigma: noun; *a person or thing that is mysterious, puzzling, or difficult to understand; a riddle.*

The lady in the office had been right, Mr. E was mysterious and he loved talking about how things are like puzzles and riddles. It was like he saw life as one big mystery to solve, and he loved piecing things together.

Puzzle Week: now it made a little more sense. He wondered what kind of puzzle they would be solving and what other mysteries Mr. E would be taking them through. School had never been quite this interesting before, he thought as he drifted off to sleep.

On Sunday night, Trent laid out the same style jeans and gray t-shirt for the morning and placed the hat on top. *I can do it again tomorrow*, he thought to himself as he climbed into bed. Piece of cake!

Chapter Six

Puzzle Week Begins

Trent walked into the classroom a little early on Monday to drop off the paperwork his mom had filled out. When he walked in, he saw an old record player spinning in the corner. He was the first student in the room. He had heard the music all the way down the hall, but it was old music he had never heard before.

"Welcome back, Trent. You're just in time for the concert!" Mr. E said and then gave him a wink while taking a bow. He grabbed a homemade pretend microphone that looked like tinfoil wrapped around a paper towel roll, cleared his throat, and began to lip sync to the smooth voice in the background. He danced around the front of the room like something Trent had seen in the old movies his parents would watch.

Trent instantly was drawn to the music even though it was way before his time. *What is this?* he thought. As if Mr. E could read his mind, he looked over his shoulder between the chorus and the verse and said, "It's Frank Sinatra, he's my favorite; isn't this great?" Then he grabbed his fedora hat off the filing cabinet, placed it on his head, and tipped it to the side before the next chorus began.

Trent nodded, unsure if he should admit he really liked this old song. He found himself humming along and then quickly stopped and went to his desk as he saw the rest of the class starting to come in. Mr. E, oblivious to the desks filling up, let the song finish before taking a big bow in front of the room and gaining a full standing ovation from his students. They loved starting the day with Mr. E's relaxed and fun personality and they never knew what they would be walking into. Trent pulled his hat down tighter and looked around the room at how relaxed everyone seemed. *This school is different*, he thought to himself. He couldn't explain it, but he thought for sure if they saw his ears the bullying would still look just like every other school.

"Okay, ladies and gentleman, as you know this classroom is an Enigma! It's a puzzle and you, my friends, are the pieces! Puzzle Week has begun!" said an excited Mr. E. "We are on a mission to find your superpowers. I hope you're ready to be discovered!"

Trent still didn't understand the puzzle pieces, or what *enigma* exactly meant, but he looked around the room and the rest of the class didn't look confused at all. This clearly was not new to them and he was going to have to catch up so he didn't stand out and get lost in the project.

Mr. E went over to the board and wrote across the top in a bright blue whiteboard marker: "Learn What You Have in Common."

Chapter Seven

Learn What You Have in Common

On the whiteboard in big letters, Mr. E wrote the focus for the first day of Puzzle Week: "Where we are similar, we come together to relate."

"This is the first part of discovering yourselves and each other. Today we are focusing on similarities or things we have in common that brings us together. This also helps us have subjects where we share interests to talk about. Then we can recognize things in our lives that help us to connect."

He explained to the class that they had an entire day filled with activities that would help them find out what they have in common. The first activity was the sticky note Speed Challenge!

Each student got a stack of sticky note paper. There were 15 different white boards set up around the room, each with a question in different categories. They were to go to each station, answer the question on a sticky note, and put their name on it. Next, they would look at the other answers, and stick their own answer to the whiteboard. If they had the same answer as someone else, they would stick it to the bottom of the other sticky note to make one long sticky note trail. One station asked, "What is your favorite food?" If you answered pizza and someone else answered pizza, then you would stick your note to the bottom of their note showing you had that in common to create a group in that category with a shared interest.

Here are some of the other questions Mr. E shared:

- *Do you have brothers, sisters, aunts, uncles, grandparents, or cousins who live with you?*

- *Do you walk, ride a bus, ride a car, ride a bike, or take the train to school?*

- *Do you prefer to read, watch a movie, play a board game, play a video game, or play a sport in your free time?*

- *Do you speak any languages besides English? (Which ones?)*

- *Have you ever struggled in a school subject? Which one?*

- *What is your favorite animal?*

- *Would you rather make something creative like art or a story, or solve a problem or a riddle?*

- *If you could be a superhero, which one would you be?*

- *Are you allergic to anything? What is it?*

- *What food do you wish you never had to eat ever again?*

The class moved through the stations and worked on their answers. Trent stopped himself at a few of the questions when he realized he was writing down his real answers instead of trying to answer what everyone might say. He quickly got back to trying to blend in and answered as plainly as possible. He was super allergic to a lot of foods. Peanuts, eggs, shellfish, plus forget about going outside when anyone was mowing the grass. But he quickly scribbled on his sticky note, NO ALLERGIES. *Only nerds had tons of allergies, right?* he thought to himself.

He got stuck at the superhero question. What superhero could he possibly be, unless Dumbo the elephant was a superhero. He snorted at his own dumb joke, which was another trait he often felt self-conscious about. Invisible, that would fix everything. *If only I could disappear*, he thought. Mr. Invisible, he wrote. Then no one would ever be able to make fun of him again.

The students began sticking their notes up on the boards and finding out who they had answers in common with. Then Mr. E made groups that matched the kids who had the most things in common.

"These will be your groups for the rest of today's activities! Get to know each other, talk about your answers you had in common, and see what else you might share as well! Report back to me at the end of the day and tell me all about each other!" said Mr. E.

Trent realized that his fake answers had paired him with a group that he had nothing in common with at all. He was already making a mess of things. His lies now meant that there was no way he could blend in and his plan totally backfired. He felt the prickly heat of panic creep up the back of his neck, which was already sweating from the tight hat he was looking forward to ripping off at the end of school. He heard the negative thoughts starting to churn in his head. "How are you going to get out of this one, Trent? You really messed up again!" He shook his head trying to quiet his thoughts before someone could notice he was getting upset. His negative thoughts were always making things worse, but he didn't know how to get his mind to stop sometimes when he was worried or anxious.

The rest of the day was spent doing activities like asking each other questions, playing guessing games, quizzing each other, and making group posters to show how much their group had in common. Even though Trent wasn't in a group that had a lot in common with him from the lists at the start of the day, he began to relax as he learned that he actually did have quite a bit in common with his group. By the last activity of the day, making posters, Trent had forgotten all about the hat squeezing his head and the stress of the morning. He had been exchanging jokes with his group until they all couldn't even finish a sentence without falling into another fit of laughter.

As Trent headed home, he even offered to carry Emma's books for her so she could dance her way home in her tap shoes. He was smiling. *This is the best school, and I have the best teacher. Blending in was definitely the secret I've been missing*, he thought. *I just had to be like everyone else and look at how much fun I had!*

But Trent remembered that tomorrow was going to be a different topic and he was getting nervous again. Mr. E said they would be finding out where they are different. He laid awake that night worried about how he could possibly get himself through this one without standing out. He woke up the next morning still hopelessly out of ideas. *Maybe blending is my superpower. Maybe I can just focus on that.*

Chapter Eight

Discover How Others See the World

Trent rolled over and buried his head under the pillow as the sun began peeking through the blinds. It had been a long restless night and his alarm clock would be going off any minute. He had no idea how to get through the day. No plan at all, and yesterday had been such a great day he was afraid to ruin everything.

As he headed to school, he kept thinking about how to choose things about himself that might be different but also not so different that anyone could make fun of him. It was his only hope at keeping this new school experience the best one yet.

Emma was wearing a costume to school. Literally, she was wearing her Halloween costume from last year, complete with the unicorn headband with a horn and rainbow tail tied onto a belt over her leggings and a bright pink t-shirt. She was prancing the entire way because she wanted to make it "realistic." Trent finally asked her why she was dressed up for school and Emma told him all about her teacher's challenge to come to school today as their best selves. She explained that when she was her best self, she always felt magical, like a unicorn, so she wanted to get into character. Trent felt a little embarrassed for her, but he felt something else that he couldn't put his finger on. What was it?

He realized what it was as he watched her prance through the parking lot to the front door of her school building. He was envious. She was so comfortable in her own skin, being her true self. All this hiding was starting to wear him down and the hat was becoming unbearably hot and a little smelly. For a brief moment he thought about taking off the hat and being himself, but he immediately thought of all the laughing and jokes at his expense at past schools and he pushed that idea out of his head and headed into class.

"Okay, class! It's another discovery day and I think this one is the most fun of all!" said an excited Mr. E. "Today we focus on how we each bring a different perspective to everything that we do. That perspective shapes how we see our world, how we see each other, what we believe to be true, and it can affect the limits we see as well. The great thing about perspective is that even in the most uncontrollable circumstances, our viewpoint can always be changed, and we can use that to change the outcome or future to something better. That's so powerful!"

Trent listened as Mr. E explained the day's agenda and realized that what they were talking about was very different from what he was afraid of. This was totally new to him, and he found himself really excited about the activities scheduled. Mr. E wrote the focus on the whiteboard for the day: "Perspective is a Superpower! The more we have, the clearer our picture of the world becomes. This builds connections and empathy."

The first activity was a giant number drawn on the pavement outside in chalk. There were also several pictures hung up around the outside of the building. They were each given a sheet of paper and a pen and were to go to each station and simply write down what they saw first. It was a timed exercise, so they had to move quickly to get to each one before time ran out.

Trent went over to the first station. It was so easy. It was definitely a 6. At station 2 there was a letter on the ground. It was an *M*. Next he went to a picture that was of a woman, and another one that was an old lady. He was racing through and wondering where the challenge was in this easy assignment. The class heard Mr. E belting out his favorite song, "New York, New York," another Sinatra song, and they knew that meant time was up. They sat in a circle and got ready to share what they wrote down at each station.

It didn't take long for the class to realize that they had not all seen the same things. The *M* was clearly a *W* to several students. The 6 was a 9 to others. The pictures looked totally different to some of the students. What seemed like an easy task suddenly felt impossible. How could they all have seen different things?

Mr. E was enjoying the chaos as he prepared to explain what was going on and, of course, make a very important lesson out of it. He knew exactly what would happen when they looked at the pictures.

"Okay, class, let's go station to station and take a look. You were in a hurry so that made this even harder but also more realistic as we often find ourselves rushing around each day with our busy schedules. Many of you saw an *M* here. But stand on the other side. What do you see now?" asked Mr. E.

A murmur of understanding was passing through the class. "Oh, I see how the 6 can look like a 9, too! Come look over here from this side!" shouted one of the students.

"That's right," said Mr. E. "And these other pictures are optical illusions. If you look at it a little longer you will see that there are actually two versions of this picture."

Chapter Nine

The Perspective Box

Mr. E got out a stack of old shoeboxes and held one up to show the class after they had all gathered under their favorite outdoor classroom willow tree.

"For the next activity, you are going to talk within your groups about the subjects in this shoe box that I wrote on notecards. Your objective is to learn different perspectives. You'll talk about how you feel about the subject and then explain why you feel that way based on an experience, something you've been told or heard, or a lesson you learned about it."

Mr. E handed Trent one of the shoeboxes and told him to take his group to a nice peaceful spot where they could get into a meaningful conversation. "Trent, I'd like you to be the leader in your group for this. Please make sure everyone has a chance to participate and that you help the quieter students get the chance to share and speak." Trent felt special to be picked as a leader. He'd never been chosen to lead anything before. He gave Mr. E a nod and was determined not to let him down as he pointed to a group of benches near the bird sanctuary and asked his group to meet over there.

As they sat down, Trent cleared his throat loudly to get their attention. "I am opening the box, guys! I'll give each one of you a card to be in charge of and then we can discuss them." The group nodded in agreement, much to Trent's relief, as he handed the cards around the circle.

Sarah went first and read her card to the group. "Mine says, Rollercoasters that spin around a lot are:

1. Really fun
2. Scary
3. Make me sick
4. Other

"Oh, for me that's going to be 3. I think spinning rollercoasters are the worst. That is based on my experience. Well, not my experience exactly, but I watched my little brother get sick on the tilt-a-whirl and it made me not want to go on it at all."

Trent nodded in agreement. He preferred the rides that went up and down and not the ones that spin around a lot, as well. He voiced his agreement and then asked for other perspectives in the circle. They got a variety of different experiences and viewpoints and then moved onto the next person's card. Each subject helped them to get to know each other on a whole new level as they shared what shaped their world and learned new ways to look at things.

Trent went last to finish up the activity with his group. He read his card out loud and then paused as he tried to decide how to answer. "Okay, my card says, making new friends is:

1. Really easy for me and I enjoy it

2. Something I dread doing and avoid

3. Easier when I know we have things in common

4. Impossible

His first instinct was to pick an answer that made him look easy to like and popular. That would be number 1 for sure, he thought. But it felt like so much of a lie that he couldn't bring himself to say it. He knew his most truthful answer would be number 2. He had made friends before but the process was difficult and something he didn't look forward to with each move. Then he was afraid of moving and losing his new friends all over again. He looked at the options again and knew which one fit the best for his experience at this school.

"I choose number 3 because when I know I have something in common with someone I feel more comfortable finding things to talk about," Trent said.

The group took turns answering and sharing their own experiences making friends. Trent was surprised at how honest many of the kids in his group were being with how hard they struggled to make friends. They all looked so confident and were really nice people. This was the most fun class he'd ever been a part of. How could they struggle to make friends like he did? His mind was spinning again. He thought he was the only one.

Vanessa, who often kept to herself and who was gone for part of the day to work with her own small group and another teacher for extra help, took a deep breath and started to share. "I have trouble making friends because of the way I process information. Sometimes I can't tell if someone is making a joke or being serious. Sometimes I just get so caught up inside my own head that I forget other people are even around. I like to talk things through out loud to myself and sometimes people think that makes me strange. I have to leave our class to work with a teacher who helps me process information and deal with things that really bother me, are a lot of distractions or loud noises around me. Sometimes that makes me feel like I'm not a part of the class or that I'm not as smart."

Vanessa was so good at math and she had even figured out the riddles that Mr. E had posted on the wall outside the classroom, Trent thought. How could she ever think she wasn't as smart? Did everyone doubt themselves like he did? He was really starting to wonder if things weren't at all what he thought.

Trent tucked the cards back into the box and found himself lost in thought as he walked over to Mr. E to turn it back in. "What's on your mind, Trent?" asked Mr. E as he took the box from his hands.

"Mr. E, I've been in a lot of schools and I've never known this much about my classmates before. And I haven't even been here a week. But I feel like I've known them forever. Why is that?" asked Trent.

Mr. E patted him on the shoulder and gave him a big smile. "That's because you're solving the MYSTERY in Mr. E's classroom. The more you learn about each other, the more you'll connect with them and form great lasting friendships, as well as the tools to understand your world better. You were a great leader today, Trent. I'm proud of you!"

Trent's eyes lit up at the praise and he realized that he really had done a good job with his group. He would have never felt comfortable getting up in front of a group and leading before. Was it the hat? Was covering his ears the secret all along? He was still lost in thought the whole way home while Emma danced circles around him in her scuffed-up tap shoes. Tomorrow for Puzzle Week they were going on a field trip to a surprise destination to interview some people. He was excited about anything Mr. E had planned. So far it had all been really fun and different from anything he'd ever done in school before.

Chapter Ten

The Field Trip

They all climbed onto the bus the next morning with notebooks, pens, and a question sheet in hand. Trent read through some of the questions while he wondered who they would be interviewing. Mr. E got on the bus last and stood in the front to talk to the class before they left the parking lot.

"Okay, guys, this is my favorite part of Puzzle Week! We are going to Wrinkle Town! It's actually called Winkle Farms, but it's where my parents live and they love to call it Wrinkle Town! It's a community for retired army veterans and their spouses when they need a little help taking care of themselves. My dad served in the war and he is now 85 years old. He lost his eyesight in one eye and his left arm, but he hasn't slowed down much! He'll challenge you to a game of ping-pong within a few minutes of meeting you, still as competitive as ever!

"What about your mom?" asked Trent. "Is she competitive, too?" He pictured Mr. E's parents having dueling ping-pong battles in the middle of an old folks home while everyone watched.

Mr. E's usual smile faded just for a quick second before he answered. He explained that his mom had been ill and didn't have a lot of time left. She was in the hospital section of the community and they would get a chance to talk to her if she was feeling up for it, but she tired pretty quickly.

"We go visit them every year for Puzzle Week and it's something they look forward to, so I know if she's up for it she will be sitting up and ready to answer questions. And, Trent, you're absolutely right. My mom is a feisty competitor. Back in her day she could take on this whole class in a game of ping-pong or just about anything and she would find a way to win." Mr. E's eyes got that sparkle back in them as he recalled those fun memories of her.

When they arrived, Mr. E led them into a large room and the residents who were going to be interviewed were each sitting at a table that had a couple extra empty chairs at each one and their name on a tent card.

They were assigned small groups they would work with to visit tables and ask questions that were assigned to their group. Each group had different people they were assigned to talk to and specific questions for each person.

Mr. E's mom was sitting up in a hospital bed they had brought down, still hooked up to some tubes and wires but looking comfortable with her nurse sitting in a chair beside her. Mr. E came over to Trent's group and said, "Since Trent has never met my parents, I made sure they are on your list. I told them all about our new student, Trent. They are excited to meet you!"

Why would they be excited to meet boring, plain me? thought Trent. But he didn't care. He wanted to meet the parents of the most interesting teacher he'd ever had. They had to be really fun!

Chapter Eleven

Are You a Giraffe?

The groups made their way around the tables asking questions like, "What is your favorite memory? What do you wish you could do over? What did you want to be when you grew up and what did you end up doing?"

Trent and his group got to Mr. E's parents last. They sat down and introduced themselves and immediately Mr. E's dad pulled out a worn ping-pong paddle to show them his favorite toy. "Still works as good as the day I got it. Me, not so much." This was followed by a raspy laugh. He looked at Trent and said, "Let me guess, you're Freddy Fafoofnick, right?" Trent looked around confused while the rest of his group laughed. James, one of his fellow group buddies, explained that he calls everyone that; it was a running joke every year.

Trent looked him in the eye and answered, "Yup, sir, that's me, but you can call me Trent!" Mr. E's dad gave him a wink and said,

"I heard you were a smart one, Trent; let's have your questions and I'll try to keep up with you!"

Trent scanned his paper for the questions he was supposed to ask:

"What do you remember the most about people who made an impact in your life?"

Mr. E's dad sat in thought for a moment and then told them how the people that made the biggest impact in his life were the ones who were the most unique. They stood out from the rest for being more honest than others, or more kind, or more caring. They went above and beyond what you expect. They had interests that were outside the box of what most people liked, and it made being around them fun, exciting, and it made life so much better to have them a part of it.

He gave a few examples and Trent was taking lots of notes to try and keep up. But his brain was on overload. Everything he was learning this week was the total opposite of what he was trying to do. Was he wrong? Why was it working if it was wrong? He hadn't been teased or bullied at all since he came to this school. But deep inside he knew that when he was being himself, he was also unique, and different, and not at all like everyone else, and he never had been. What if that made him special? He shook his head as though to get rid of these thoughts and refocused on his note taking.

They had a question for Mr. E's mom as well:

> "What do you wish you could change about something growing up now that you look back at it?"

She answered in a softer voice, clearly having to put effort into speaking with an oxygen tank helping her through it. "Oh, that is one of my favorite questions and I hope you take this to heart, young ones. I wish I had let people see the real me. I spent a lot of time hiding things I thought weren't perfect and it kept me from really connecting with people. Sometimes it held me back from trying exciting things. But really it just stole a lot of my energy that I could have put into making this life and this world the best it can be. Now I celebrate who I am, but I wish I had learned that a lot earlier. I could have saved myself a lot of misery and missed opportunities.

"You see, I realized that people are going to judge us no matter what. They will think what they want to think based on their own perspective. They may see me as a 9 or a *W*, but if I know I'm a 6 or an *M*, then what they think doesn't matter. They may say I'm a giraffe! But I wouldn't go run and check the mirror to see if it's true because I already know that it isn't.

"You see? When you know who you are and the value you bring to this world with the same certainty that you know that you are not a giraffe, then no one can change your truth. If it's not a doubt that you allow in your own mind, then you'll never be limited by the doubt that comes from someone else. When you know who you are and how your uniqueness adds flavor, excitement, and purpose to this big world, then you can focus your energy on being that person to the best of your ability, instead of questioning if you're good enough or trying to hide.

"What other people think will never change your truth, good or bad. Choose carefully what you believe about yourself!"

She reached into a bag next to her and pulled out a small figurine of a giraffe and handed it to Trent. "Trent, are you a giraffe?" she asked him and looked right into his eyes.

Trent shook his head as he closed his hand around the gift. *I'm not,* he said in his mind. Then he returned her gaze and said with a tiny hint of confidence, *"I know I'm not."*

Trent wasn't taking notes anymore. He wasn't even moving as what she was saying started to hit home like nothing he'd ever heard before. He was quiet the rest of the day, even through dinner download, and he laid in bed that night still processing what Mr. E's mom had said to them. The giraffe figurine was sitting on the nightstand and he drifted off that night staring at it, wondering why Mrs. E's words had hit something so deep inside of him.

Chapter Twelve

What's Under Your Hat?

"Okay, class! It's time for 'What's under your hat!' so let's all get in a circle over here in our chat space under the tree!" said Mr. E as he lifted the needle off the record player spinning more of his favorite Sinatra tunes.

Trent hadn't slept well but he was pretty sure he just heard Mr. E say something about what's under a hat and he was getting worried about what this activity would be. So far Mr. E hadn't asked him about his hat since the first day. He was hoping he'd forgotten about it but now he wasn't so sure.

Mr. E looked around the circle at the class and explained the activity. "What's under your hat is just a figure of speech. This is an opportunity to share what's going on between your ears, under your hat. In other words, what's on your mind today! What are you thinking about, worried about, excited about, stressing about, confused about . . . you get the idea. This is where we can share anything we need to get off our chest in a safe space and support each other."

Trent was going to be last to go and he couldn't think of anything he wanted to share with the group. His anxiety was starting to grow as he sat and waited. But something happened as he listened to his classmates unpack what was on their minds. He was again seeing how everyone in class had fears, insecurities, doubts, and hardships, just like he did. Just because they seemed happy in class didn't mean they weren't going through their own things, too. He had been so worried about his fears that he hadn't stopped to think about what everyone else might be facing in their own lives.

Jen shared her concerns about her gymnastic meet this coming weekend. She'd been working really hard but twisted her ankle coming down wrong on the balance beam last week and she wasn't sure she'd be able to compete. She needed to finish well at this meet to get to the next level and it was all she could think about lately.

Chris shared that his aunt had moved in to help take care of him. His mom was having some problems and needed to go get some help and he was worried about her. He was embarrassed to tell anyone about it but it had been really hard to focus at school.

Grace stood up, in typical dramatic Grace fashion, and she pulled a bandage off her cheek. "Okay, guys, I can't stand this thing on my face anymore. I've had this zit all week and I pretended I cut myself because

I didn't want anyone to know but it keeps getting bigger and bigger and I hate it!" The class got really quiet and then started to laugh. "Grace, I can't even see it!" said Jen. The rest of the class reassured her that it was completely not noticeable and then started talking about their own pimples and pimple stories. "Has anyone seen that pimple popping show?!" asked Chris. A bunch of groans and laughs broke out as they all knew what he was talking about: the show on TV about gigantic zits being popped.

Mr. E looked over at Trent, who was clearly in deep thought about something. "Trent, you're up. What's under your hat today?"

Trent stood up and looked around at his classmates. They had all just shared really vulnerable concerns and struggles. They had been honest and real, and all week had been fun and kind to him. He felt bad that he had been hiding his true self. He was feeling less afraid of showing them what he'd been hiding under his hat, but still those old teasing memories were not far away in his mind.

Chapter Thirteen

No More Hiding

"There's, ummm . . . There's something I want to do, and I just don't want anyone to laugh at me," said Trent shyly from his spot in the circle. All eyes were on him and he was feeling butterflies swirling around inside. He was worried that he was about to ruin everything, but something inside him told him that he didn't feel right hiding anymore.

The class got really quiet as Trent pulled at the snaps at the back of his dad's hat. He took a deep breath and slid the hat off of his head, freeing his smashed ears from their misery. He lifted his eyes to see the reaction of his classmates. They were silent and staring right at him. A feeling of dread started to creep in.

"TRENT!" shouted James. "You're not BALD?!"

Trent stood still for a moment. Then he started smiling. His smile turned into a laugh and his laugh turned into the entire class falling over laughing into the grass.

"You thought I was bald?" Trent tried to ask between laughs.

Chris looked at Trent wiping away tears from laughing and asked him, "What was with the hat; I don't get it." The rest of the class echoed his question, not sure what he was trying to show them.

Trent looked at the class, who all seemed very interested in the story behind the hat. "Well, my ears, I didn't want to be made fun of for them anymore, so I wore the hat to hide them."

"What's wrong with your ears?" asked Jen. "I don't get it."

Trent pulled out his phone to look at them. Maybe the hat had pushed them down for good! But he peeked at his reflection and they were the same old ears he always had. Big, sticking out all over the place.

Mr. E smiled at the class. He explained to them, "When you are connected to each other and when you learn to look for and appreciate the traits people have, the heart they have, and get to know their amazing personalities, then you see and value the whole person. You don't look at things to judge or make fun of, like if someone has a pimple, or a different shaped nose, or ears, or if they walk different, or stutter sometimes, or don't wear the coolest clothes or listen to the music that everyone else listens to. Those are superficial things we focus on when we don't take the time to learn about what really matters and who people really are. Trent, if you had taken that hat off and actually been bald, I am willing to bet the class still wouldn't have teased you. Because in just a few days they have already learned so much about you and love having you here with us. We haven't laughed like this all year! You are so much fun and a great leader, too. Your ears just make you look like Trent! And we appreciate them because they are a part of you, and we appreciate you!"

Trent was processing everything Mr. E was saying, as he looked around the room at his new friends. *Was he right?* Trent wondered. He hadn't judged the other kids in class for how they were unique or different from him because they were such fun people. He had accepted them right away and actually found their uniqueness to be the best part. He was enjoying this class and this school because it was like nothing else he'd experienced. But they didn't have these ears. Little doubts still circled in his mind as he reached his hand into his pocket to hold onto the little giraffe figurine he now carried around with him everywhere.

Mr. E told them about the last day of Puzzle Week coming up and the trip to a museum. He called them all in to the middle of the circle and had them put their hands in to make a promise and do their class cheer. "Everything we just shared is safe in this space and we will use this information only to support and lift each other up to become our best selves and grow stronger together! Mystery on 3, guys, ready?

"1. 2. 3. MYSTERY!"

Chapter Fourteen

The Museum

The bus was extra noisy on the way to the museum as the excitement for another adventure was building. They drove past a large stone building, one of the most well-known museums in the area, but the bus didn't slow down. They passed another one, and another, and James finally spoke up.

"Um, Mr. E? Are we going to any of the museums downtown? We passed all the science buildings already," he said as the driver turned down a little driveway just outside of town.

Mr. E gave him a big smile and told the class they weren't going to any ordinary museum. "The museums downtown are really quite incredible and we should definitely go back to those another day. Today, we are going somewhere a little different. Is it really a Mr. E adventure if we go somewhere ordinary?"

The bus pulled up in front of a small brick building with an engraved silver sign hanging from a chain over the front. It was covered in vines and little purple flowers. The sign said The Museum of Inimitable History.

Trent tried to read the sign. He'd never seen that word before. "Mr. E, what's In-Inim-iniminiminbul mean?" The class laughed as they all had the exact same question, but no one could seem to pronounce it.

Mr. E threw his head back and laughed at the word he often struggled to get out without being tongue-twisted himself. He cleared his throat and he said in his most dictionary-sounding voice, "Inimitable. *In-imit-a-ble*. Adjective. So good or unusual as to be impossible to copy; unique. This is a building dedicated to the superpowers of people who have created and accomplished incredible things. But not only did they make history by what they did, they did it with people doubting them. With traits that made them unique. With plenty of reasons to make excuses or quit, but instead they had courage and embraced who they are, and that, my favorite super-students, is why they are not only amazing, but inimitable! This is about the power to embrace your uniqueness, to unleash your best qualities and talents as a gift to the people around you by defeating self-doubt. And, that, my friends is how you unlock your authentic greatness so you can share it with the world. Just like you will see that these inimitable superheroes have done for us."

Trent's mind was racing. He thought this was just about the greatest word he'd ever heard. He hadn't thought about the things that made him different, the very things he wanted to wish away, to avoid being bullied for, being anything other than something to hide. What if those things were actually what made him more special? What if it truly did add value to be your authentic self that no one else could possibly copy? He was still trying to sort out this new way of thinking. The puzzle, the enigma, the riddle of it all was beginning to make sense piece by piece. But the old doubts and negative thoughts were cluttering his ability to grasp it fully. He wasn't ready to accept the truth that was beginning to flesh out right in front of him.

As they filed into the little old building, his mind was beginning to open to new ideas. He couldn't wait to see who had made the cut for the museum of inimitable history and just what was so special about them on top of all the great things they accomplished.

Chapter Fifteen

The Museum
of Inimitable History

An energetic man dressed head to toe in purple came out from behind a desk and greeted the class in a thick Russian accent. "Welcome, welcome friends, to the museum. It's unlike anything you have ever seen before. Here we celebrate achievement, yes, like many other museums. But, more important, we celebrate the person behind the achievement and how they are unlike any other!"

He bowed to the class and tiptoed backwards away from them, opening the path to start the tour. He turned in a full circle and then approached them again as they started walking, making them all stop short in their path and bump into each other like bumper cars. The class laughed; this guy was going to be a fun tour guide.

He began to speak again but this time he had a thick Italian accent. Trent looked around at the group. They were as entertained as he was. "Um, sir, did your accent change?"

"Yes, yes, smart boy, I am fluent in over 20 accents." He replied with a wink and a smile.

Jason spoke up next, "Do you mean languages?"

"Oh no, I mean accents. I don't even speak English so good!" he said with a laugh, quickly switching to a southern American accent.

Mr. E was so glad his friend Drew was still the owner of this amazing museum. He was always full of fun, full of great knowledge, and as inimitable as you can be, which made his tours the best in the world. He explained to the class that their amazing tour guide, Drew, used to do voice-overs for some great producers out in LA, but he moved back home to open this unique museum, a dream he always had.

Drew took them to the first exhibit. It was Albert Einstein. He asked the class to tell them what they knew about him. The students remembered that he was a great physicist who developed the theory of relativity and is known for being a brilliant mind. Einstein is a household name people recognize for being incredibly smart even if you don't study all the things he contributed to our understanding of physics and motion.

Drew looked at the class, "But,'" he said, "did you know that he wasn't always considered so brilliant? He didn't even speak until he was four years old or read until he was seven. His teachers and parents thought he was slow, and he wasn't considered a bright child. But he knew better. He found what interested him and he pursued it with everything he had and turns out, he's brilliant! He just hadn't found where he shined yet!"

Vanessa raised her hand, "Um, Mr. Drew, I just wanted to say that I didn't start talking until kindergarten. I am autistic and I had a really hard time adjusting to school, but once I started being able to communicate better, I was able to catch up in a lot of things. My mom said that my teacher was concerned that I would struggle to keep up in school because I had trouble learning, but I have straight *As* this year." Vanessa beamed. She was realizing how much it meant to her to show people what she could accomplish when they tried to put limits on her that she knew didn't fit. Her straight *As* were a big source of pride for her because she knew how hard she had to work to complete some of the assignments that were outside of her comfort zone. It felt good for her to finally talk about her learning struggles and social skills challenges with her class this week. She was tired of hiding the fact that sometimes it was hard for her and her class was making her feel comfortable to finally be herself.

Drew looked at Vanessa and pointed right at her. "You, my friend, may find yourself with your own exhibit in this inimitable place one day! You certainly have the makings of an inimitable achiever!"

Trent suddenly wanted to be in this museum one day. He knew he wasn't like anyone else. Why was he suddenly getting excited about all the things he'd been trying to hide?

The group walked over to the next exhibit. "This," said Drew, "is a singer named Stevie Wonder. He's written and performed many famous songs you've probably heard before. He won three consecutive Album of the Year awards alongside another singer that I think maybe Mr. E might be familiar with: Frank Sinatra!

"As though his achievements weren't already enough to land him in the Museum of Inimitable History, he also did all this without his eyesight. He played the most incredible songs on the piano all without the benefit of being able to see what he was playing. He did it all by listening."

One by one they went through the exhibits, and with each one Trent was getting more and more restless with his thoughts. Mr. E could see he was wrestling with something heavy and he remembered all too well the moment he realized just how special his own unique traits really were. He remembered that moment when he felt free to truly be himself and how much that meant to him. Trent was learning what the rest of the class had been learning all year long and the "aha moment" was imminent. It was inimitably imminent. He was proud of Trent for really engaging in Puzzle Week and knew that he'd started on his way to discovering himself and his best life.

Once they were back in their classroom at the end of the day, Mr. E asked Trent to hang out for a minute before he headed home. "Trent, how did you like the museum today?" he asked him.

Trent was still deep in thought, and he looked Mr. E in the eyes and said, "Mr. E, this has been the most unique week of school I've ever had. I think maybe tomorrow you're going to meet someone you haven't met yet. I need to think about this some more. I really like that word. *Inimitable*. I can't stop thinking about it."

Mr. E gave him a smile. "You're doing some great inner work, Trent. I think you're going to get it all figured out. Look forward to seeing you tomorrow as we finish out

Puzzle Week. Do you think you'll know your superpower?"

Trent smiled. "Yes sir. I already have it. I'll tell you tomorrow!" and he headed out to get Emma and walk her home.

Chapter Sixteen

Emma

Trent showed up at Emma's building, but the usual tap-dancing wonder was nowhere to be seen. He looked all over the parking lot to see if she was off dancing with her friends or jumping around on the playground, but she wasn't there either.

He heard some faint sniffling from over by the stairwell, so he made his way over and peaked down the steps. That's where he found Emma, sitting on the steps with her head in her lap and her tap shoes in a pile at the bottom of the stairs.

"Oh, hey, Emma. Umm, you okay?" Trent was shocked to see his usually happy and carefree sister upset. He walked down the steps and grabbed her tap shoes and tucked them in his bag and held out his hand to help her up. "Come on, buddy, let's go home, okay?"

Emma looked up, eyes swollen, and face drenched with tears and she nodded.
She seemed a lot sweeter when she was

struggling, thought Trent as he worried if she was okay. He hadn't seen her like this before and he thought whatever it is, she must be really upset because nothing ever bothered this kid.

They headed around the last corner to the house and Trent finally asked Emma what was wrong. She started tearing up again and told him that one of the kids at school said her tap shoes were annoying and some of her classmates put up signs petitioning to make her stop wearing them at school. Then the teacher had agreed that they were a little distracting and loud during the school day.

"And then, and then, they all started talking about my tap shoes and how I shouldn't be allowed to wear them in the building and then someone said I'd never be a good dancer anyway and I never want to go back to school because they all hate me," she ended with a giant sob.

Trent felt a pang of empathy. Even though he had thought he wanted her to experience what bullying felt like because she didn't seem to understand why he struggled so much, when it came down to it, he didn't want anyone to feel that kind of hurt.

In that moment, another thought hit him. Mr. E had been trying to teach him this all along. The reason Emma was not affected by teasing the way he was, was because she was so confident in who she was. She knew she was special. She had fun being uniquely herself. She didn't take comments from others to heart. She wasn't a giraffe and most of the time, she knew it.

But he had struggled relentlessly because his negative thoughts and doubts had always felt validated by the comments and teasing he heard from others. He let other people decide his worth, his value, his limits, and even how he felt about himself. His reaction made it more fun for them to tease him even more, and then he would go home and wonder if everything they said was true. This whole week he had been learning to be what Emma had been all along. Confident in who he was, appreciating the unique traits in himself, and also recognizing the amazing value of the unique traits in others. Emma, he thought, just needed to remember who she was, the authentic greatness she freely shared with the people around her every day.

"Emma, they said things about you before that weren't that nice. They called you the new clown girl and that didn't bother you at all. You thought it was funny. Why didn't you get upset then?"

Emma answered right away, "Because I knew I wasn't a clown and I picked that outfit because it was funny. But I really want to be a tap dancer. I want to practice all day and

I want to become really, really good! But they said I'm not good."

Trent stopped walking and looked at Emma. "Emma, it didn't bother you because you knew what they said wasn't true. You're letting your own fears and doubts be confirmed by what others think or say. You're allowing yourself to believe that what they are saying is true. Just do what you did before. You know you are a great dancer! The best I've ever seen, anyway. You practice every day and work really hard to get better. That belief is what determines if other people's opinions matter, affect us, or define us. And we know they don't! That's your superpower! You are unshakeable! You live as the best Emma every single day and you love who you are. Even though it's hard to believe right now, your friends at school love you for who you are, too."

Trent reached into his pocket and grabbed his little sister's hand and shoved the tiny giraffe figuring into her palm. He told her what Mrs. E had shared about knowing we are not a giraffe and the certainty we must have about who we are so that others cannot cast doubts in our hearts.

Emma's eyes lit up as she looked at the giraffe. She clipped the small figure onto her necklace, gave Trent a big hug, and grabbed her tap shoes out of his bag. "I'm wearing these home. Because I'm the best dancer you've ever seen, and you won't want to miss my new moves!" she shouted and then started dancing her way up the driveway.

Trent felt good about sharing the lesson that had meant so much to him this week. He shouted out to her, "HEY EMMA! Are you a giraffe?"

She spun around and yelled back with all the confidence she could muster, "NO WAY!"

Trent could hear her singing all the way into the house, "I'm not a giraffe, I'm a DANCERRRRRRR!"

Chapter Seventeen

Becoming the Most Extraordinary Kid

That night, Trent looked at the assignment they had been given to work on going into the last day of Puzzle Week. Across the top of the paper it said this: "I Am Unique Because (make a list of everything you can think of!)."

Trent started to fill his paper out. He'd been so focused on blending in that at first he was having trouble remembering what he actually liked. He paced around the room and then wrote down, "My ears are probably the coolest ears anyone has ever had; no one has anything like these!"

He smiled, knowing no one could copy those, at least not without a good plastic surgeon! But what else? He wandered down to the kitchen to get himself something to drink and found his mom and sister sitting at the table talking to his dad on the iPad.

"Hey, guys; hey, Dad," he said as he grabbed a glass from the cabinet.

"Hey there, T-man! How's the new school going?" asked his dad.

Trent told them about the assignment he was working on and how he was having trouble finding what made him unique. His family quickly assured him they had him covered, and he pulled up a chair and got his pen ready to write.

"You walk me to school, and I don't know any other brothers who will do that in my school! And you come to all my dance recitals," volunteered Emma.

He looked down at the paper and wrote:

I support and take care of my little sister.

"What about your music? You make those great tracks on your computer and you've even had people pay you to create some for them! That's pretty special!" said his dad from the iPad.

Makes songs and music for bands, and I started my own business.

"Your closet! Trent, you have the best coordinated outfits I've ever seen. Well at least until this school anyway. Coordinated from head to toe and your sneaker collection in every color without a single scuff mark," said his mom.

Always dressed in the best.

He was starting to think of more now that he was hearing ideas from his family and he was trying to write faster to keep up with his brain.

I play every sport I can sign up for: golf, basketball, tennis, soccer, baseball, weightlifting, archery, volleyball, and the list will keep growing because I want try them all. My favorite car is a black 1979 El Dorado and my favorite singer is now, after being introduced by Mr. E, Frank Sinatra and his song "That's Life." I love old movies and anything that has to do with Italy. I have an Italian flag on my wall that my grandmother sent me, and it is my favorite gift. I have a jar filled with birthday and Christmas money I have been saving to go to Italy one day with my best friend and neighbor from the first town I lived in as a kid. I miss my dad. A lot. He's always at work and showing up on a screen, but I am grateful that he always makes an effort to stay connected even though it makes my family a little different. I had friends at my last school that didn't always have enough to eat at home, and I brought extra sandwiches to school to make sure they got lunch. Sometimes I would take half my dinner and wrap it up and bring it to them the next morning. I've known I wanted to help people, to do big things, even when I was a little kid. I had big dreams and goals that most people thought were crazy.

As Trent sat there thinking, he realized that the people he got along with the best were always the ones who were dreaming big dreams, taking big actions, and working toward some big projects. He loved having friends who were different than everyone else; it was one of his favorite traits in other people. Being unique. Just like Mr. E's parents had talked about when they shared who the most memorable people they met were. He hadn't thought about that until this assignment. He loved being around other motivated people who weren't afraid to fail and who wanted to do great things that would have an impact on people. Impact. He was unraveling the mystery the deeper he went into this new way of thinking. It wasn't enough for him to be inimitable so that he was truly unique; he wanted to also use that uniqueness to make a difference like the people he learned about in the museum.

An inimitable impact, he thought. *That's what I want to create with my life! I want to make a difference like no one else can, because there is only one me.* He thought about the times he was bullied, the hardships of moving and making new friends, of missing his dad and seeing how much work his mom put in to fill that void. He felt the joy in making the connections he made this week and the new self-love he was finally learning to have, and he experienced another new shift. Gratitude. He was excited for school the next day. He knew exactly what he was going to do and for the first time in his life, he knew who he was and who he was working to become.

On the wall the first day of school, Trent read the words, *What is YOUR SUPERPOWER?* He had been confused by the idea behind Puzzle Week then, but he understood it now. Being able to have confidence and embrace everything that made him who he is would give him the power to unleash and share it with everyone he met. That made his uniqueness a superpower, for his own life and the people he would be able to affect with it.

Chapter Eighteen

Becoming Inimitable

The alarm clock went off almost an hour before the usual time Friday morning and Trent bolted upright. He'd been waiting for morning to come for what seemed like weeks. Today was the day he celebrated all that was Trent and all that would be. But more than that, he wanted to celebrate everyone, every unique trait and colorful addition that each person brought to his world. He was filled with a gratitude for all things that were the total opposite of what he'd been trying so hard to become: plain.

He thought hiding himself would bring happiness, but it made him feel sad, trapped, and miserable. The freedom in allowing himself to simply be who he truly was gave him a peace he'd been seeking for a long time and he wanted to help others feel that way too by encouraging them to be themselves and share it!

He opened his closet and beamed. *I missed this colorful display of perfection*, he thought. He grabbed the exact outfit he had planned in his head and carefully put it all on, feeling more like himself than he had in a long time. On his way down the stairs, he stopped in Emma's room.

"Hey, Emma, I need a favor. Can I borrow something?" he asked her as she was tying the ribbon on her tap shoes. He explained exactly what he needed and why and she grinned ear to ear. "It's in the closet, Trent! You can keep it, it's perfect for you!" she said and then tapped her way down the wooden steps, clicking on each one.

Trent pulled a piece of paper out of the printer and with a marker he carefully wrote

MR. INIMITABLE across the page. He cut around the letters and used some safety pins to secure them onto the back of what he had grabbed out of Emma's closet. He was ready. He'd never been more ready in his life.

He showed up a few minutes early, partly to catch the end of Mr. E's Sinatra routine but also because he wanted to arrange a special entrance to class with his teacher. Mr. E was belting out the chorus to one of his favorite songs when he caught a glance of Trent standing in the doorway.

"Hello there, Mr. Trent! I almost didn't recognize you! Tell me what brings you in so early this morning?" asked Mr. E. Trent walked into the classroom and explained his plan and showed Mr. E his finished list from last night's assignment. Mr. E was so proud of Trent and his transformation in just a week. He nodded and they made a plan and Trent headed out of the room for the big reveal.

Chapter Nineteen

Mr. Inimitable Has Arrived

The class sat in their seats chatting with each other and waiting for Mr. E to start class. A few of them looked around wondering where their new friend, Trent, was this morning.

Mr. E stood up and made his way to the front of the room and announced that they had a new student coming today. The students all looked at each other wondering why they had another new student in the same week already. And where was Trent?

He went over to his record player and before he put down the needle he looked at his students, a sparkle in his eye, and he read off Trent's list.

"My students, a mysterious new person is coming to join us today. But you know him and you all love him. You just maybe didn't know him as well as you think. Here are a few things about him that may surprise you."

Mr. E read through the list. The mysterious introduction was keeping everyone's eyes glued to the door wondering what was going on. He dropped the needle down on the record and "That's Life" started playing in the background. The lights flipped off and when they flipped back on there was a figure standing in the doorway. With a cape.

Mr. E turned on the floor fan, making the cape ripple in the wind. Then he said in his most Hollywood voice, "Presenting, Mr. Inimitable. Trent Inimitable."

There he stood, in the best superhero pose that he could muster. Cape blowing behind him with the name Mr. Inimitable pinned onto it. Black, spotless basketball shoes with red laces. Black shorts. A red polo with black stitching. And his backwards red hat with the word IMPACT across the front. His ears, however, weren't pinned back like before when he was trying to hide who he was. The hat went right behind them, making them stand out even more against his silhouette.

He let out a nervous laugh and the class started clapping, first awkwardly but it turned into a full standing ovation.

Something about Trent owning who he was, and all his uniqueness, made them feel proud, excited, and somehow relieved about being their own unique selves. There was a freedom for them in Trent's decision to be comfortable in his own skin.

Chapter Twenty

Story Time with the Soccer Team

"And," said Mr. Inimitable, also known as Coach Trent, "As the song came to an end, Mr. E gave me a nod to go ahead and share what I said I would like to talk to the class about. I asked them to join me under the tree outside. As they gathered around me in our favorite spot, I told them about my experiences moving and being teased. I told them why I wore the hat and the plain clothes at the beginning of the week.

And then I did something that made Mr. E so proud that he told me he knew it was a moment he would never forget as a teacher. I went around the circle and shared what I thought was unique and special about each person in the class."

"Coach, what happened to the teacher, to Mr. E?" asked Meredith.

Mr. Inimitable smiled and looked over to the tree behind the field where he had spent that morning telling his class about his struggles and recognizing their superpowers. "Let's walk over to the tree and we can finish practice there," he said, leading them to a spot that he'd cherished for so many years.

"This plaque on the tree wasn't here when I was a student," he said. "We put this up five years ago when Mr. E passed away to always remember the lives he touched and the love he poured into all of us with his mysteriously fun teaching and Puzzle Week, which we still do, to this day!"

"Is that why this is called the Mystery Tree?" asked Michael, suddenly putting it all together. "That's right, Michael! We named it after our favorite teacher!" replied Coach.

"Coach, is Emma the dancer everyone has been talking about who is in that new show in New York? Is that your sister?" asked Sarah, who was an aspiring dancer herself.

"That's right, Sarah, that is my amazing sister! She knew she was a great dancer and she never let doubt get in her way again. She's still the best dancer I've ever seen," he said with a smile. "Now, before I send you on your way, it's time to share your superpowers!"

Each member of the team stood up and took a turn sharing what they believed was their superpower. One said Encouragement. Another said Caring. One said Patience. Another said Dedication. And around it went until it was Meredith's turn. Meredith was twisting a clump of grass into a knot as she tried so hard to come up with her superpower, but she couldn't think of anything.

Mr. Inimitable smiled, remembering all too well that feeling of being disconnected from his true self and how powerful it was to embrace everything that made him unique and special and have something of value to contribute.

Coach Trent was excited to tell the team the last rule of Puzzle Week that was especially designed for a group or team and would bring them together with a united purpose.

"Okay team, there is one more part to Puzzle Week that I saved for last. That's rule 3: 'A team filled with teammates who use their superpowers to lift each other up cannot be defeated.' We are an inimitable team, and to be unmatchable we have to know exactly what makes us so unique. That means each person brings something of value that we appreciate, want to help develop and grow, and that we will hold each other accountable to. So, I need your help. Everyone here has a superpower and Meredith can't see hers. What can we do?" he asked his team.

Michael stood up, inspired by the way Mr. Inimitable had told his classmates how each of them were special back when he was a student at their school, and how he was such a great leader. He looked at Meredith and said, "You have a lot of superpowers, Meredith. You're always the hardest worker, even when you don't know anyone is looking."

Jeremy, the goalie on the team, thought about a time that he didn't think he had much to offer his teammates and how much that bothered him. He didn't want Meredith to feel that way and he jumped up next to Michael to add his thoughts. "Meredith, Michael is right. But you also always offer to help people on the team when they need to work on something instead of getting frustrated that they aren't doing well. That's a great superpower!"

Shannon remembered a time she didn't have a ride and Meredith had walked with her all the way home. She jumped up with her teammates and nodded and said,

"Meredith, you walked me home that time I didn't have a ride and no one else would have done that. You're always looking out for other people."

One by one, the team each started sharing superpowers they saw in Meredith and her heart was so full from the love she received from her teammates. She didn't even know they noticed any of these things she did. Mr. Inimitable reached into his bag and pulled out a slightly faded red cape with letters that were now officially stitched onto the back that read, Inimitable. He tied it onto Meredith and the team started to fan it, making it blow in the wind.

"Introducing, the new Ms. Inimitable!" said their coach. Meredith had never felt this special just for being herself before. She made her best superhero pose and coach pulled out his phone and played his favorite song as loud as the phone would go.

"Okay, guys, lets clean up the cones and get out of here!" Meredith said and then ran to the field, cape flying in the wind and the team laughing as they competed over who could grab the most cones.

Coach could hear the team bantering back and forth about parts of the story he had just shared.

"Who here is a giraffe?" he called out to them. "NOT ME!" came the replies. "I like giraffes!" said another voice "That's not the point!" "I want to be a puppy!" The fun continued all the way to the parking lot.

Coach Trent looked over at the plaque on the tree and smiled. "Thanks, Mr. E," he said out loud and touched the letters on the engravement:

> I am Enigmatic. A mystery. And so are you. And the journey to finding, embracing, appreciating, and valuing our true selves and the uniqueness in each other is the most worthwhile adventure of them all. May you all be found to be Inimitable, and on a mission to leave an Inimitable Impact on everyone you meet.

Discussion Questions

Chapters 1–3: The New Kid

Trent struggled in the past to fit in with kids at school and dreads the bullying he is certain will be repeated at his new school. He is focused on the areas where he thinks he is different from his peers and believes that hiding them will make people like him more.

Think of a time you were the new person and didn't know anyone.

What group was it with or what type of situation was it?

What were you most worried about?

What did you feel the most confident about?

Do you remember what you first noticed in your first interaction with this group of people? How would you describe how comfortable you felt?

Have you ever had an experience when someone made you feel special for something that makes you unique or when they made you feel self-conscious because you are different in some way?

Chapters 4–5: Meet Trent and Emma

Although Trent dreads meeting new people because of negative past experiences, Emma seems unaffected by the opinions of others. Trent is focusing on areas of himself that he feels bad about, and Emma is focused on having fun in the moment.

Do you identify more with Trent or Emma when it comes to being yourself?

Do you think you spend more time focused on the present moment, worried about the future, or about what others will think of you in interactions that are coming up?

Anxiety and excitement send the same signals from your brain. The difference between the two is the meaning we assign to that feeling. Do you think you tend to feel more anxious or more excited before trying new things or meeting new people? Elaborate on your answer.

Trent struggles with his mind racing as he worries about the future. What are some things Trent can do to stop focusing on his fears?

Chapters 6–7: Puzzle Week: What We Have in Common

Mr. E explains to the class that their commonalities bring them together and enable them to find ways to relate to one another.

Think of a group you are in and list as many things as you can that you have in common with other members of the group.

What are some ways you can learn more about your group members to find the areas where you have similarities?

What questions can you ask to get to know your group members on a deeper level to have more meaningful conversations about shared ideas and experiences in your life?

Chapters 8–9: Puzzle Week: Discover How Others See the World

The students are taught that the perspectives of others help us see a more complete picture of the world around us. They also learn that what we see is combined with what we already know to form our truth. That means that learning the viewpoints and experiences of others is an important part of creating our reality.

How can you learn more about the way others see the world to understand their perspectives?

What is the value in learning more about the people in your group or team?

Do you think that your relationships would be stronger if you knew more about the experiences, ideas, and opinions of the people in your group or team?

Chapters 10–15: Puzzle Week: Field Trips

The Inimitable Museum teaches the students that not only do we each have our own unique traits but also others who have done some amazing things had to learn to embrace their own uniqueness along their journey and use them as a superpower instead of an excuse.

Think of three people you would consider to be successful either in your field of work or in some area you have an interest. Look them up and find out what traits they have that make them one of a kind and impossible to copy.

Mrs. E tells Trent that he must believe positive things about himself with the same amount of belief that he is not a giraffe so that the opinions of others do not affect what he can do and who he can become.

What are some doubts and fears that consistently come into your mind when you try to do something challenging, are about to meet new people, or when you attempt to accomplish a new goal?

What is a goal that you wish you could try, or that you have tried to accomplish on several occasions, that you are not yet able to conquer?

What do you think is keeping you from trying or completing this goal?

Can you identify a limiting belief in the form of a doubt or fear that plays a role in holding you back?

What would you tell yourself, as if you were talking to a cherished friend, that would give you encouragement and fill yourself with positive belief to overcome those negative thoughts?

What are some ways you can remind yourself of those positive beliefs each day until you believe them with the same conviction that you are not a giraffe?

Chapter 16: Helping Others: Everyone Has Doubts Sometimes, Even Emma

For the first time, we see Emma lose confidence and doubt herself. Trent uses the lessons he is learning to help others and realizes he can do more than embrace his own unique traits.

Why does Emma start to doubt herself?

How is Trent able to turn her thinking around to help Emma find her confidence again?

What could you do to lift others up and help them restore confidence in themselves?

What specific things can you say to people you know who are experiencing doubts in who they are or what they can accomplish?

Chapter 17: Embracing and Identifying Our Unique Superpowers

Trent is starting to understand that his unique traits might be a good thing. But he can't embrace them until he really gets to know himself. To embrace your own uniqueness, take some time to explore who you are.

Make a list of what makes you inimitable. List your traits, likes, personality, background, unique perspectives, experiences that shaped your view of the world, etc. No two people in the world will have the same list. Discover what sets you apart.

Can you think of a time one of these traits helped you overcome a situation or reach a goal?

Which traits do you think others tend to recognize as strengths when they get to know you and how has it helped when working with others to add to the team's overall goals?

Chapters 18–19: Unleashing Our Authentic Self

Once Trent identifies and celebrates his own uniqueness, he must face his fear to unleash his authentic greatness into the world. That means he will be vulnerable to the thoughts and opinions of others if he leaves any room for doubt in his mind.

How do you think it felt for Trent to finally be himself with his class?

How was Trent able to use this experience to not only be true to himself but also to lift up his classmates as well?

Trent shows confidence and kindness when he becomes Mr. Inimitable. How do you think this helped his classmates embrace his uniqueness and also feel comfortable enough to share their own uniqueness and confidence?

Chapter 20: Inimitable Teams Lift Each Other Up and Cannot Be Broken

Coach Trent finishes telling his story about becoming Mr. Inimitable to his soccer team. He remembers his old teacher, Mr. E, and then passes the Mr. Inimitable name onto a new student.

How big of an impact do you think Mr. E made on all the students who were a part of his class? Do you think you could make that kind of impact with the people you interact with in your life? How?

When you figure out what your superpower is, how can you use that to lift others up and contribute it to everything you do?

When you understand the true power behind your uniqueness, how does that help you to feel confident in yourself so that doubt, negative thoughts, and opinions of others do not become a limiting belief?

Do you know what your superpower is? Do you think you can have more than one?

How can you show others appreciation for their superpower and encourage them to use it?

What can you do when you hear someone saying something mean about someone else because they are "different" to help shift their perspective and embrace differences as a gift?

What can you do each day to remind yourself that you are inimitable and to share your greatest gift with the world?

The Original
Mr. Inimitable

I was searching for a word to describe the idea of embracing our uniqueness, our differences, and valuing the different perspectives and experiences that have shaped who we are. That's when I met my friend Trent and he introduced me to his favorite word: *inimitable*.

In a world with so much division we need more to shape our reality than simply seeing through a singular lens that we see as truth. There must be another option than eliminating anything that doesn't fit the mold or blend with the group. Self-doubt and fear of being called out for not thinking or living the same as the people around us has created more self-limitations and has the potential to sabotage us from becoming our authentic selves more than anything else.

I was introduced to Trent Witz though Twitter where I learned about what Minneapolis North High School is doing for students who play basketball. The introduction was through a documentary piece he was sharing. A high school where these incredibly gifted athletes rarely considered college and most didn't complete their education and graduate has been transformed through the work of passionate coaches like Trent Witz and Larry McKenzie.

Minneapolis North became a powerhouse of basketball, gaining national attention for recruiters because the coaching staff had turned a school that some officials said needed to be shut down into a school with a basketball program carrying 100% graduation rate.

These student athletes now consistently continue their sports careers at a two- or four-year college because some coaches were on a mission for positive change and turned this into a program for hope and not just about a game.

Trent, single dad to Emma and Trent Jr., quickly showed me what a driven person can do with a passion for elevating the lives of kids within a community. He isn't just director of operations for the program, or an assistant coach involved on the sidelines when he had time. He continually invests in the community as a part of the Minnesota Black Basketball Coaches Association, and working with countless community programs, he has connected the team to powerhouse organizations such as the Minnesota Timberwolves, organized tournaments, fundraisers, and meals for kids who needed them.

Trent Witz with his children, Emma and Trent Jr.

Trent has mentored these kids through heartbreaking challenges including the heightened civil unrest Minneapolis has been navigating over the past couple of years. Mid-season 2022, one of the honor roll standout student athletes on the Minneapolis North Basketball and football teams was a victim of senseless gun violence, leaving the team devastated and coming together to mourn a fallen teammate. The coaches of this program organized quickly to rally support in a city that's been rocked by violence. They passionately provide hope to these growing young men who have experienced far too much harsh reality.

Trent is known in Minneapolis and the basketball community for his dedication and time with these kids. I wondered how someone could accomplish the things that he gets done to serve others as well as the enormous amount of time and support he pours into his own kids, and the answer didn't take long for me to discover.

Trent is inimitable. I do hope that others will try to imitate him because they would be giving back to their communities in a way that will have a powerful impact on the next generation. But I know that no one will be able to serve quite like Trent does, and his kids are learning the value of giving their best self to others as well. If you drive past his car, which reads INMTBL across the back, or hear a little Frank Sinatra playing from the stereo, or perhaps hear someone talking about making it to Italy one day, then you'll know you've found him. The original Mr. Inimitable.

Along with my friend and inspiring colleague, we created a podcast highlighting the inimitable impacts of some pretty amazing people such as Damon West, Lea B. Olsen, Jamie Yuccas, Dave Conord, Janine Tucker, John Thomas, and more.

We started a movement: a quest to embrace our quirks, our views, our personalities, and give ourselves permission to be proud of who we are and where we are like no one else. That is how we can leave an impact on this world to create a positive ripple in a way that no other person can—because no one else is just like us.

Trent showed me the superpower that comes from recognizing when we feel different or like we don't fit the mold and responding with genuine gratitude.

"You think I don't fit in? Well, that's because I am INIMITABLE! Thanks for noticing!"

And if you look at all the incredible traits, knowledge, experiences, beliefs, dreams, and purpose within yourself, then you will find that you are INIMITABLE, too! Your superpower is waiting on you to embrace it, and then unleash your authentic greatness as a gift to the world and the people you encounter.

Resources

If you are interested in a keynote or workshop based on *Superpower*, visit superpowerthebook.com or email info@ kateleavell.com.

Visit superpowerthebook.com for info on these topics:

    Downloadable activities

    Book club materials

    Posters

    Videos

    Bulk orders

    Meeting real-life people sharing their inimitable superpower stories

    Sharing your story

About the Author

KATE is a speaker, workshop facilitator, and bestselling coauthor of *Stick Together*, written with Jon Gordon. She is a former NCAA and high school lacrosse coach, corporate sales consultant, and coaches' education trainer. She is the VP of leadership development for the Jon Gordon Companies and helped to create workshops, collegiate leadership academy curriculum, and a teen leadership program based on Jon Gordon's bestselling books. Kate works with teams and leaders around the world to boost performance, connection, and energy. She is passionate about teaching strategies that turn a powerful vision into reality while unifying teammates around their purpose and mission. Kate is also the author of *Confessions of an Imperfect Coach* and the *Emergency Coach's Guide* for girls' lacrosse.

Kate is an 8 year survivor of a pulmonary embolism. Through her talks and writing, she shares the "plus one" mentality of living each day focused around gratitude and purpose. She believes that each day is a gift and another opportunity to experience life and explore our greater purpose.

About the Illustrator

Jay Schwartz is an accomplished illustrator/cartoonist, graphic designer, and art director. He has created illustrations for children's books, websites, e-books, products, and packaging. He lives in New York on Long Island with his family.

You can view more of his work at www.jayschwartzcreative.com.